FAREWELL
TO THE
WESTERNS

Farewell to the Westerns

A PICTORIAL TRIBUTE TO THE BR'S CLASS 52 DIESELS

Edited by Geoffrey Kichenside

DAVID & CHARLES

NEWTON ABBOT · LONDON · NORTH POMFRET (Vt) · VANCOUVER

Other recent titles by Geoffrey Kichenside
STEAM
BRITISH RAILWAY SIGNALLING

ISBN 0 7153 7069 3
Library of Congress Catalog Card Number 75-10699

Printed in Great Britain
by Alden & Mowbray Ltd Oxford
for David & Charles (Holdings) Limited
South Devon House Newton Abbot Devon

Published in the United States of America
by David & Charles Inc
North Pomfret Vermont 05053 USA

Published in Canada
by Douglas David & Charles Limited
132 Philip Avenue North Vancouver BC

BR's class 52 diesels – the Westerns

When the detail of the 1955 railway modernisation plan was being evolved there was still enough independent thought at the Western Region's Paddington headquarters to produce reasoned arguments sufficient to force the then British Transport Commission to agree to the development of diesel-hydraulic traction for WR services instead of diesel-electric locomotives planned for the rest of the country. Thus were evolved what became the well-known Warship and later the Western classes for principal passenger services, and other types for secondary and local workings. This album is devoted to one of those classes, the Westerns, also known as the D1000s or the class 52s, depending on which of the various official identities you prefer. The Westerns were really the WR's top line diesels for express passenger trains, but they were equally at home on heavy freight haulage. The photographs portray Western class locomotives at work on many parts of the WR and have been assembled from a variety of sources. This book does not set out to describe the technical aspects, for this has been done already in *Diesel-Hydraulic Locomotives of the Western Region* by Brian Reed, also published by David & Charles.

The Western class diesels were notable in many ways, not least in their names, which to the non-GW/WR fraternity smacked so much of pompous disregard for authority at 222 Marylebone Road and everyone else with such titles as *Western Enterprise, Western King* and *Western Ruler.* One name, *Western Independence*, remarkably, was omitted, yet these locomotives epitomised the last fling of that traditional spirit of Great Western independence, nearly 15 years after the GWR had been brought into the nationalised British Railways. Not only did the WR convince the BTC of the desirability of building the Western class diesel-hydraulics to fulfil the need for a higher-power type than the Warships, but, because it was necessary to complete the class quickly and capacity at Swindon was limited, part of the order was placed with Crewe. It was almost akin to the LNWR building a batch of GW Stars!

The main batches of Westerns entered service in 1962/3 and soon after allowed the final programme to eliminate steam traction on the WR to get under way. When delivered the first few Westerns sported various liveries including desert sand, green and maroon, but the latter colour was eventually adopted as standard for this class, contrasting with green used for other BR types, until blue became the new standard for all motive power from the mid-1960s.

The Westerns have always been associated mainly with the West of England services, largely because for most of their lives they were allocated to Laira depot, Plymouth, for heavy maintenance, but they also took an important share in London-Bristol/South Wales duties and, as part of their diagrams from Laira, worked between Paddington and Birmingham, and for a time, until withdrawal of through services, to Birkenhead as well. Indeed one of their earliest functions was to provide the extra power needed for the heavy Paddington-Birmingham trains until completion of the LMR Euston-Birmingham electrification in 1967 took the pressure off the WR route. They have also performed duties on the Bristol- Birmingham line, even working through occasionally on Midland territory to Derby. Because of their basic 'belonging' to the WR, workings away from former GW routes have not been widespread and the few regular workings and casual appearances in other parts of the country have usually ranked as noteworthy in enthusiast circles simply because the class has not had the same universal use of comparable diesel-electrics.

Moreover the locomotives were also limited by their ancillary equipment; for example not until half way through their lives were they fitted with the BR standard automatic warning system in addition to the GW type with which they started life, and at the same time they were provided with train airbrake equipment. They were not fitted for providing electric train heating since they had no generators of the capacity of the diesel-electric locomotives and were thus not able in winter to work electrically-heated stock, or at any time the fully air-conditioned sets which were drafted to Paddington-Bristol/South Wales services in 1973 and effectively reduced their range of WR passenger duties. In emergencies however they were not unknown at the head of air-conditioned trains, though with what effect on passengers deprived of ventilation other than by opening the drop windows in the doors at the coach ends, has not been recorded.

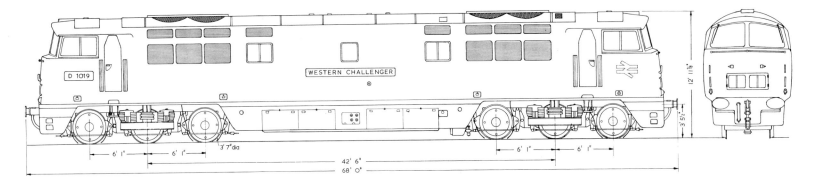

It was perhaps inevitable that the WR diesel-hydraulic classes would not last long. They did not really have the blessing of the BRB and since the entire hydraulic fleet accounted for only about 11 per cent of all BR diesel locomotives it was hardly surprising that they were regarded as non-standard and the 1967 national traction plan envisaged early withdrawal. The Westerns were the last to go but they were a long time a-going: as these notes are written about half the class remain active. Indeed despite growing unreliability because of a maintenance run-down in their last years they often had to turn out to replace ailing diesel-electrics which were supposed to have ousted them. Even to the end the WR often seemed to prefer a Western diesel rather than a diesel-electric on its Golden Hind and Cornish Riviera expresses.

Now they are going they have an affectionate place in the interests of many enthusiasts, although not perhaps to the extent of their Castle and King predecessors; the standardised Western Region, brought into line after almost 30 years of nationalisation, will not be the same any more.

Farewell, Westerns. You were born unloved into a steam age world. You had your troubles, but once your needs and temperament had been understood you did well and have an honoured place in the motive power history of the West.

The class 52s — technical details

Length over buffers	68ft
Length over body	65ft
Width overall	9ft
Weight in working order	108 tons
Wheel diameter	3ft 7in
Engines:	Two Maybach MD655 pressure-charged V-type of 1380bhp at 1500rpm
Maximum engine output	1760bhp
Transmission:	Two Voith/NBL L630rU triple torque convertors
Tractive effort:	Maximum starting 72,000lb continuous 45,200lb at 14.5mph
Maximum speed	90mph

The class 52s — names and numbers

No	Name	Date in traffic	No	Name	Date in traffic	No	Name	Date in traffic
1000	Western Enterprise	20/12/1961	1027	Western Lancer	29/1/1964	1054	Western Governor	2/3/1963
1001	Western Pathfinder	12/2/1962	1028	Western Hussar	29/2/1964	1055	Western Advocate	2/3/1963
1002	Western Explorer	19/3/1962	1029	Western Legionnaire	14/7/1964	1056	Western Sultan	8/3/1963
1003	Western Pioneer	14/4/1962	1030	Western Musketeer	5/12/1963	1057	Western Chieftain	6/4/1963
1004	Western Crusader	12/5/1962	1031	Western Rifleman	20/12/1963	1058	Western Nobleman	25/3/1963
1005	Western Venturer	18/6/1962	1032	Western Marksman	31/12/1963	1059	Western Empire	6/4/1963
1006	Western Stalwart	6/7/1962	1033	Western Trooper	17/1/1964	1060	Western Dominion	11/4/1963
1007	Western Talisman	1/8/1962	1034	Western Dragoon	15/4/1964	1061	Western Envoy	19/4/1963
1008	Western Harrier	4/9/1962	1035	Western Yeoman	27/7/1962	1062	Western Courier	6/5/1963
1009	Western Invader	24/9/1962	1036	Western Emperor	29/8/1962	1063	Western Monitor	17/5/1963
1010	Western Campaigner	15/10/1962	1037	Western Empress	31/8/1962	1064	Western Regent	24/5/1963
1011	Western Thunderer	27/10/1962	1038	Western Sovereign	7/9/1962	1065	Western Consort	18/6/1963
1012	Western Firebrand	17/11/1962	1039	Western King	7/9/1962	1066	Western Prefect	14/6/1963
1013	Western Ranger	3/12/1962	1040	Western Queen	20/9/1962	1067	Western Druid	18/7/1963
1014	Western Leviathan	24/12/1962	1041	Western Prince	10/10/1962	1068	Western Reliance	12/7/1963
1015	Western Champion	21/1/1963	1042	Western Princess	19/10/1962	1069	Western Vanguard	21/10/1963
1016	Western Gladiator	16/2/1963	1043	Western Duke	26/10/1962	1070	Western Gauntlet	28/10/1963
1017	Western Warrior	15/3/1963	1044	Western Duchess	12/11/1962	1071	Western Renown	7/11/1963
1018	Western Buccaneer	2/4/1963	1045	Western Viscount	16/11/1962	1072	Western Glory	7/11/1963
1019	Western Challenger	2/5/1963	1046	Western Marquis	24/12/1962	1073	Western Bulwark	3/12/1963
1020	Western Hero	21/5/1963	1047	Western Lord	4/2/1963			
1021	Western Cavalier	17/6/1963	1048	Western Lady	15/12/1962			
1022	Western Sentinel	16/7/1963	1049	Western Monarch	24/12/1962			
1023	Western Fusilier	23/9/1963	1050	Western Ruler	1/1/1963			
1024	Western Huntsman	1/10/1963	1051	Western Ambassador	21/1/1963			
1025	Western Guardsman	1/11/1963	1052	Western Viceroy	4/2/1963			
1026	Western Centurion	24/12/1963	1053	Western Patriarch	11/2/1963			

All locomotives carried D prefix until the end of steam traction on BR. Letter D painted out or removed from numberplate since 1968

With an exhaust that would grace any steam locomotive No 1005 *Western Venturer* eases out of
Paddington with the 11.30 to Penzance, the
latterday Cornish Riviera Express, on 23 May 1974.
K Connolly

A feature of working at Paddington since the
abolition of steam and the rebuilding of the station
has been the ability of trains to arrive and depart
from most platforms instead of the original
segregation in which broadly speaking most arrival
trains used the platforms on the east side and
departures on the west side with only a few in the
middle accessible from up and down tracks. Here
No 1018 *Western Buccaneer* winds its way across
to platform 4 with an up train from Paignton on 2
June 1973. *K Connolly*

One of the original functions of the Western class was to provide the extra power for the generally heavy trains on the Paddington, Birmingham and Wolverhampton service which was usually beyond the capacity of the 2000hp Warship class if a reasonable speed level and reserve for delays was to be maintained. At the time when the Western class was introduced the Paddington-Birmingham line was about to assume a major role carrying all traffic between the two cities because the rival LMR service from Euston had been cut temporarily to allow major engineering works to be undertaken as part of the electrification programme for the West Coast main line. On completion of electrification in 1967 the Euston route became the major inter-city service from Birmingham while the WR route concentrated on maintaining a useful link between such places as Reading, Oxford and Banbury with Birmingham. Moreover as part of rationalisation in the Birmingham area all inter-city traffic was concentrated at the rebuilt Birmingham New Street station and the former Great Western station at Snow Hill was closed. *Above* No 1003 *Western Pioneer* winds through the platform loop at West Ruislip with the Sunday 16.10 Paddington-Birmingham train on 9 June 1963. *C R L Coles*

Top right Western Prefect leaves Birmingham New Street with the 12.25 to Paddington on 9 November 1974. *K Connolly*

Bottom right The same train, but photographed on 29 June 1974 in the charge of No 1044 *Western Duchess*, takes the tortuous path round the spur from the Euston line to the Midland Camp Hill line at St Andrews Junction before taking yet another spur at Bordesley to reach the former Great Western Paddington line. *K Connolly*

Above An unidentified member of the class speeds over the graceful flat arches of Wharncliffe Viaduct near Hanwell crossing the River Brent with a down express on 7 October 1971. *P R Foster*

Top right No 1021 *Western Cavalier* emerges from Sonning cutting with a Paddington-Bristol train on 10 October 1964. *Gerald T Robinson*

Bottom right One of the regular Western freight duties, particularly in their last years, was the working of stone trains from Merehead Quarry on the Witham-Cheddar branch to various parts of Southern England. One of the workings of these trains went to Ardingly near Haywards Heath on the Southern Region and often a Western class locomotive would work through to Redhill. Here No 1064 *Western Regent* heads down the relief line alongside the former Moreton Yard near Didcot with returning empties to Frome on 2 February 1974. *Gerald T Robinson*

Above Three Western class diesels stand side-by-side in Swindon Works, No 1001 on the left under repair and two others nearing completion on 17 March 1963.
G A Richardson

Top right After some particularly ugly results in the front-end design of some of BR's earliest diesels the BR industrial design team took a hand in shaping the front end of the Westerns to overcome the box-like effect sometimes seen on diesel locomotives with the cab right at the front. Although the general shape sloped back from buffers to roof the angled front windows set back from the body panels, and the forward upsweep above the windows to meet the slope of the roof, gave the Westerns a distinctive appearance quite unlike any other BR diesel type.
Barry J C Hillmer

Bottom right A comparison between the front ends of the Western class on the left and the Hymek class on the right.
Barry J Nicolle

No 1014 *Western Leviathan* coasts down the 1 in 68
gradient on the South Wales main line between
Patchway tunnel and Pilning with a fitted freight
train on 14 June 1970.   *P J Fowler*

The driver of No 1015 *Western Champion* eases off
through the cutting approaching Stoke Gifford ready
for the slight speed restriction through the junctions
of Bristol and South Wales main lines near what
today is Bristol Parkway station, with the 17.00
Paddington-Swansea train on 7 July 1970.

P J Fowler

An unidentified class 52 heads a Bristol-Paddington train up the gentle slope climbing away from Bristol towards Keynsham in 1969. *P J Fowler*

No 1072 *Western Glory* coasts into Bath Spa with a
Bristol-Paddington train in the mid-1960s. After the
initial livery experiments the Western class locomotives settled down for a time to maroon livery with
the BR coaching-stock type insignia which can be
seen here at the leading right hand end.

G F Heiron

Above A panoramic view of Bristol Temple Meads
in August 1967. No 1026 *Western Centurion*, newly
painted in blue livery with full yellow front end,
winds its way round the curves south of the station
with a North of England-Paignton train. *G F Heiron*

Left On a fine summer afternoon in August 1964
the 15.15 Bristol-Paddington climbs steadily up the
steepening grades towards Box tunnel. The locomotive, believed to be No 1039 *Western King*, is fitted
with the circular rotating windscreen panel instead
of more conventional wipers, an experiment tried on
a number of BR locomotives at that time but not
then pursued. *G F Heiron*

Above No 1021 *Western Cavalier* coasts over the junction west of Reading to join the Bristol line with an up West of England-Paddington train on 15 September 1973.   *K Connolly*

Right Snow billows up in a cloud as a class 52 sweeps through Thatcham with the 9.55 Paignton-Paddington on 1 February 1972.   *D E Canning*

The 13.30 Paddington-West of England train passes through Hungerford in 1968. The station is no longer like this today since after the 1972 freight train derailment here which demolished the signalbox the new signalbox was built on the platform on the left-hand side.   *D E Canning*

A late evening shot of No 1023 *Western Fusilier* on royal train duty seen here passing Newbury in 1969. The locomotive and leading coach represent contrasts in oldest and newest, since the locomotive was built in 1963 and the coach over 50 years before, and now the oldest passenger-carrying vehicle still in use — albeit very specialised use — on British Railways.   *D E Canning*

Above No 1072 *Western Glory* sweeps round the curve of Westbury avoiding line to join the original route via Westbury station, at Fairwood Junction with a Paddington-Paignton train on 4 June 1974.
K Connolly

Top right Another view of Fairwood Junction, also on 4 June 1974, with No 1073 *Western Bulwark* taking the Westbury station line with a Penzance-Paddington train. *K Connolly*

Bottom right A day earlier No 1041 *Western Prince* approaches Fairwood Junction signalbox with a Paignton-Paddington express. *K Connolly*

A little further west from the Westbury cut-off is a similar one avoiding the town of Frome. The station loop is often used for diverting freight trains off the main line to avoid delaying passenger trains should there be any likelihood of a hold-up in getting stone trains to and from the Merehead Quarry branch at Witham. No 1054 *Western Governor* approaches Clink Road Junction at the east end of the Frome loop with a Paddington-Paignton express on 1 June 1974.

K Connolly

Clink Road Junction signalbox with No 1058
Western Nobleman passing at the head of the 11.30
Paddington-Penzance Cornish Riviera Express on
25 November 1973.   *P J Fowler*

No 1031 *Western Rifleman* takes the Frome station loop with an empty stone train bound for Merehead on 1 June 1974. *K Connolly*

No 1069 *Western Vanguard* is diverted on to the
Frome loop to free the main line for an overtaking
passenger train with empties for Merehead on 5 June
1974.   *K Connolly*

An out of the way pint-size halt known as Dilton Marsh is an important boundary point on British Railways since it forms the meeting of the Western and Southern Regions on the Salisbury-Westbury line. No 1066 *Western Prefect* runs through Dilton Marsh Halt with a Westbury-Fareham stone train on 30 May 1974.

K Connolly

On the former Midland Birmingham-Bristol main line
No 1035 *Western Yeoman* approaches Cloddy Bridge
near Cheltenham with the return empties of the clay-
liner working from the Stoke-on-Trent area to St
Blazey in Cornwall on 27 November 1973.

Barry J Nicolle

Witham station on the Paddington-Penzance main line, seen here on 3 September 1966 and closed to passengers a month later. No 1065 *Western Consort* passes with a Paddington-West of England express.

D H Ballantyne

Witham today with the single track branch to
Merehead Quarry, also to Cranmore and the East
Somerset Railway Depot, curving away to the right.
No 1001 *Western Pathfinder* heads an up relief
Penzance-Paddington train on 10 August 1974.

K Connolly

A class 52 with the 7.30 Paddington-Penzance train takes the short climb approaching Somerton before dropping down to the flat expanse of Sedgemoor and the broad River Parrett Valley on 17 November 1973.   *P J Fowler*

Another view of the 7.30 Paddington-Penzance at
Somerton on the snowy morning of 26 February
1974.   *P J Fowler*

A striking shot of No 1062 *Western Courier* as it passes Clink Road Junction near Frome with a Paddington-Penzance train on 5 June 1974.

K Connolly

No 1055 *Western Advocate* winds through the curves at Castle Cary with the 12.30 Paddington-Paignton on 10 August 1972. The now single track branch diverging to the right leads to Weymouth and until the building of the through Berks & Hants line in the early years of the present century was the only route here, forming the Chippenham-Weymouth main line.

P J Fowler

The photographer pointed his camera the other way at Castle Cary to take this shot of No 1014 *Western Leviathan* heading the 11.55 Paignton-Paddington on 11 August 1972.   *P J Fowler*

A class 52 heads the 12.30 Paddington-Paignton over
Somerton Viaduct on 12 September 1973.

P J Fowler

No 1046 *Western Marquis* takes advantage of the slight drop through Somerton before tackling the climb towards Brewham Summit near Witham with the 6.35 Penzance-Paddington on 17 November 1973.   *P J Fowler*

An unusual view of the flyover at Cogload Junction east of Taunton with a class 52 heading a West of England-Paddington train diverted via Bristol on 10 March 1973. The down line from Bristol to Taunton is carried over the girder bridge by the embankment approaches and the up and down lines of the direct Berks & Hants line between Taunton and Reading pass underneath the girder bridge to curve away to the right on the far side. *P J Fowler*

No 1042 *Western Princess* passes the remains of
Creech St Michael Halt between Taunton and
Cogload Junction with a West of England-Paddington
train on 11 October 1971.   *G T Heavyside*

Above No 1059 *Western Empire* stands at Taunton with the 15.30 Paddington-Penzance on 21 November 1973. On the far side of the station a diesel multiple-unit is about to leave for Bristol.   *G T Heavyside*

Above right No 1039 *Western King* passes Taunton with an oil train for the West of England on 11 October 1971.   *G T Heavyside*

Bottom right No 1034 *Western Dragoon*, last of the Crewe-built batch to be put in traffic, approaches Taunton from the west with an up train for Paddington on 11 October 1971.   *G T Heavyside*

No 1038 *Western Sovereign* eases over the level
crossing at the north end of St Davids station as it
arrives at Exeter with the 13.30 Paddington-Penzance
on 31 August 1972.   *G F Gillham*

No 1022 *Western Sentinel* arrives at Exeter St Davids
with a Penzance-Paddington train on 19 June 1974.
On the far platform a diesel multiple-unit waits to
leave for Barnstaple.   *K Connolly*

Although much of the surviving mechanical signalling
on the Western Region consists of relatively modern
standardised WR-pattern components, some signalling
antiquities still survive, as for example this group of
down starting signals at Exeter St Davids facing the
driver of No 1069 *Western Vanguard* waiting to
leave with an express for Paignton on 8 April 1972.
D Griffiths

Few passenger trains now pass Exeter without
stopping but some still do on summer Saturdays, as
for example the 10.56 Paddington-Penzance
relief seen here in the charge of No 1029 *Western
Legionnaire* on 29 September 1973.   *David M Cross*

The driver of this class 52 opens up as he rounds the curve at Dawlish Warren with the down Cornish Riviera Express on 24 August 1970. The footpath on which the people are walking at one time was a siding extending from the station in the far distance used for unloading wagons of stone for sea defences.

D E Canning

No 1052 *Western Viceroy* accelerates past the site of
the closed Exminster station with the 12.30
Paddington-Paignton on 16 July 1973.

G F Gillham

There would not have been much of a view of the coast from the train on this day as No 1021 *Western Cavalier* heads a Paddington-Penzance express along the sea wall near Dawlish on a misty 18 August 1973.

David M Cross

No 1028 *Western Hussar* looks rather the worse for
wear as it passes Newton Abbot with the 13.30
Paddington-Penzance on 19 November 1973.

G T Heavyside

The south end of Newton Abbot with No 1009 *Western Invader* taking the through road with the 12.40 Penzance-Paddington on 19 November 1973. The buildings in the background behind the signal-box form the offices of David & Charles Ltd, publisher of this book.

Barely three years old No 1048 *Western Lady* in
maroon livery passes Gas Works Sidings between
Torquay and Paignton with the down Torbay
Express for Kingswear on 4 September 1965.

A M Yeates

A brace of class 52s with the Ambassador escorting his lady. Nos 1048 and 1051 draw away from a signal check at Aller Junction bound for Laira, Plymouth, and are overtaken by a diesel multiple-unit for Paignton on 11 June 1974.   *Derek Cross*

A few minutes before the previous picture was taken
No 1010 *Western Campaigner* headed the 13.30
Paddington-Penzance past Aller Junction overtaking
BR/Sulzer No 46 049 with a ballast train bound for
Paignton on 11 June 1974. *Derek Cross*

Surmounting the summit at Dainton a class 52
emerges from the tunnel as the driver prepares to
shut off for the steep descent past Stoneycombe
Quarry to Aller Junction. *Marion Canning*

The classic view of the eastern slope of Dainton bank
with No 1041 *Western Prince* passing Stoneycombe
up distant signal as it tackles the final climb towards
Dainton tunnel with the 13.30 Paddington-Penzance
on 1 June 1973.   *G F Gillham*

No 1023 *Western Fusilier* drifts down past Hemerdon Sidings as the driver prepares to brake for the two miles falling at 1 in 42 towards Plympton on the descent from Wrangaton summit on the southern slopes of Dartmoor with an unfitted freight on 19 July 1972.   *G F Gillham*

Looking anything but imperial and badly in need of
a visit to the paint shop No 1036 *Western Emperor*
makes its way alongside the Plym estuary from Laira
Depot to Plymouth station to work an up passenger
train on 15 June 1971.   *C Plant*

Another shot on 15 June 1971 bordering the River Plym: No 1005 *Western Venturer* approaches the outskirts of Plymouth with an express from Paddington. *C Plant*

No 1046 *Western Marquis* passes through Plymouth
with an up mixed freight on 9 October 1974.

K Connolly

No 1018 *Western Buccaneer* but with nameplate missing and obviously having suffered slight collision damage to its bodyside panels, speeds the 14.50 St Erth-Kensington milk train alongside the Plym estuary soon after leaving Plymouth on 15 June 1971.   *C Plant*

No 1017 *Western Warrior* swings off the main line into the loop platform at Par with the Saturday 9.50 Paddington to Newquay on 14 July 1973.

D Griffiths

At the other end of Par platform on that very wet
14 July 1973, a little while before the photograph
on the previous page was taken, No 1054 *Western
Governor* arrived with the 9.30 Paddington-Penzance.
It is seen here restarting to tackle the short, sharp
climb out of the station to cross the Harbour branch
before the five miles of climbing to the summit at
Burngullow.   *D Griffiths*

Below No 1022 *Western Sentinel* heads the 10.25 Penzance-Bradford, The Cornishman, at Crugwallins near the closed station of Burngullow between St Austell and Grampound Road on 23 June 1973.
C Plant

Left At the same location the pioneer member of the class No 1000 *Western Enterprise* heads the 8.00 Bristol-Penzance, also on 23 June 1973.
C Plant

Above An immaculate No 1065 *Western Consort*
waits at Penzance ready to work the Fridays only
17.45 to Manchester on 1 September 1972.

G F Gillham

Top left No 1043 *Western Duke* arrives at Truro with
the 7.30 Paddington-Penzance on 24 October 1973.

J C Hillmer

Left End of the line from Paddington viewed across
the buffer stops at Penzance with No 1048 *Western
Lady* backing out after its train has been drawn from
the platform on 24 October 1973. *J C Hillmer*

The end of the line for some Western class 52 locomotives as they are cut up at Swindon scrapyard on
9 April 1974. In the foreground are the cabs and
part of the frame of No 1020 *Western Hero* while in
the background the breakers have just started on No
1002 *Western Explorer*.   *Barry J Nicolle*